# DOMINOES

Series Editors: Bill Bowler and Sue Parminter

# Pebbles on the Beach

## Alex Raynham

Illustrated by Ben Hasler

Alex Raynham is a writer, editor, and teacher trainer who has written a number of books for Oxford University Press, including titles for *Oxford Bookworms* and *Oxford Read and Discover*. Alex and his wife, Funda, live in Southern Turkey, and they usually spend the summer at the beach. They both like beach pebbles – so there are a lot of pebbles in their house!

OXFORD
UNIVERSITY PRESS

# Story Characters

*Abby*

**Aunt May**

**Dad**

**Mom**

*Diego*

*Bianca*

*Sadie*

# Contents

## BEFORE READING

**1** **Match the words with the pictures. Use a dictionary to help you.**

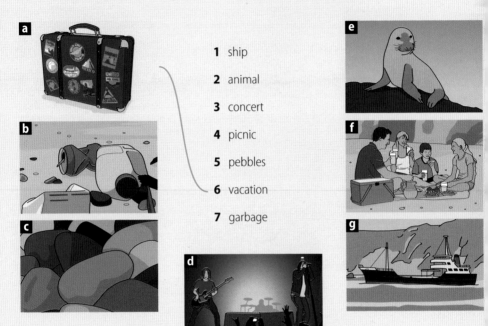

**1** ship

**2** animal

**3** concert

**4** picnic

**5** pebbles

**6** vacation

**7** garbage

**2** **Abby is from Dallas. What do you think she does in her summer vacation in California? Tick three things.**

**a** ☐ goes on a ship

**b** ☐ learns about animals

**c** ☐ goes to a concert

**d** ☐ has a picnic

**e** ☐ picks up garbage

**f** ☐ meets an old friend

**g** ☐ stays in a hotel

**h** ☐ finds some pebbles

**3** **Who is Abby often with on this vacation? Tick three boxes.**

**a** ☐ Mom

**b** ☐ Dad

**c** ☐ Aunt May

**d** ☐ her friend Sadie

**e** ☐ Diego

**f** ☐ Diego's cousin Bianca

# Pebbles on the Beach

QUICK STARTER 250 HEADWORDS

# OXFORD
UNIVERSITY PRESS

Great Clarendon Street, Oxford, OX2 6DP, United Kingdom

Oxford University Press is a department of the University of Oxford.
It furthers the University's objective of excellence in research, scholarship,
and education by publishing worldwide. Oxford is a registered trade
mark of Oxford University Press in the UK and in certain other countries

© Oxford University Press 2012

The moral rights of the author have been asserted

First published in Dominoes 2012

2020

11

ISBN: 978 0 19 424948 5    Book
ISBN: 978 0 19 463903 3    Book and Audio Pack

Printed in China

This book is printed on paper from certified and well-managed sources

ACKNOWLEDGEMENTS

*Cover image*: Corbis (Stacking stones/Michele Constantini/ZenShui)

*Illustrations by*: Ben Hasler/NB Illustration

*The publisher would like to thank the following for their kind permission to reproduce photography*:
Alamy Images p.26 (Point Reyes National Seashore/Niels van Kampenhout); Corbis
pp.27 (Jumeirah Beach Hotel in Dubai/Blaine Harrington III), 27 (Shopping mall/Roger
de la Harpe); Getty Images pp.15 (Oil slick on beach/Ben Osborne), 26 (Oil slick on beach/
Ben Osborne), 27 (Driving over sand dunes/Gerard Brown), 27 (Dubai skyline/photography
Matthijs Borghgraef); Oxford University Press pp.11 (Beetle/Photodisc), 26 (Clock on
pebbles/Gareth Boden), 26 (Beetle/Photodisc).

Abby is from Dallas. It's the **summer vacation**. She's in her room with her friend Sadie.

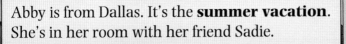

Sadie says, 'Let's go to a **concert** next week.'

'I can't,' Abby says. 'Dad's working in Dubai for DeepOil for three weeks, and Mom's going with him.'
'What about you?' Sadie asks.
'I'm staying with my **Aunt** May in California,' Abby says. 'I don't want to go, but nobody listens to me!'

**summer** the hot time of the year

**vacation** days when you do not go to school or work

**concert** people play music at a concert

**aunt** your mother's (or father's) sister

Next week, Aunt May drives Abby home from the airport in her **crazy** old car.

In Aunt May's house, Abby finds a lot of **pebbles** in her room. 'They're all different,' her aunt says. 'Your mom and I are sisters, but we're different, too!'
'What *am* I doing here?' Abby thinks. 'My aunt's crazy!'

**crazy**  not looking usual, not thinking well

**pebble**  a little round stone

## READING CHECK

**Match the parts of the sentences.**

**a** Abby's dad is …

**b** Abby's friend Sadie wants …

**c** Abby doesn't want …

**d** Abby's mom …

**e** Aunt May …

**f** In California, Abby finds …

**g** Aunt May is crazy, …

**1** meets Abby at the airport.

**2** to stay in California.

**3** is Aunt May's sister.

**4** Abby thinks.

**5** in Dubai for three weeks.

**6** to go to a concert.

**7** a lot of pebbles in her room.

## GUESS WHAT

**What do you think happens in the next chapter? Read the sentences and write *Yes* or *No*.**

**a** Abby phones her dad and says, 'I want to come home.' ..................

**b** Abby sees some interesting animals.
...................

**c** Aunt May and Abby have a nice day out.
...................

**d** Abby meets a nice boy. ...................

Three days later, Sadie calls Abby. She tells her all about the concert. Abby listens quietly. She cries after she puts down the phone.

When she goes into Aunt May's **studio**, her aunt says, 'I'm going into town for **paint** this afternoon. Do you want to come?'
'No, thanks,' Abby says. Suddenly Aunt May cries, 'Be careful! My new picture!'

Now there's black paint on Abby's best **pants**. She runs angrily out of the studio and away.

**studio** a room where people paint pictures

**pants** trousers

**paint** colour that you put on paper to make a picture

When she stops, she's on the **beach**. A boy is putting something into bags there.

'What are you doing?' she asks him.
'**Picking up garbage**,' he answers.
'When **birds** eat it, it kills them.
'I'm Diego,' he says. 'And you're staying in May Wilson's house.'
'How do you know?' Abby asks.
'We're **neighbours**!' Diego says.

'Do you want to help me?' he asks.
'OK,' Abby answers.

**beach** the land next to the sea

**pick up** to take something in your hand

**garbage** things that you do not want any more

**bird** an animal that can fly through the sky

**neighbour** a person who lives in the next house

They walk on the beach, talk, and pick up garbage. Abby forgets the paint on her pants.

When it's time to go home, she says, 'Let's meet here again tomorrow.'
'No, let's go to the **national park**,' Diego says.
'My **cousin** Bianca works there. She can take us.'
'Hmm ... **maybe**,' Abby says.

**national park** a large piece of beautiful land that the government looks after

**cousin** the son (or daughter) of your mother's (or father's) sister (or brother)

**maybe** perhaps

## READING CHECK

**Choose the correct words to complete the sentences.**

**a** Abby's *mom* / *friend* calls her.
**b** Abby is *angry* / *not happy* after the phone call.
**c** Aunt May wants to take Abby *to the beach* / *into town*.
**d** Suddenly there's paint on Abby's *pants* / *shoes*.
**e** Diego is picking up *pebbles* / *garbage* on the beach when Abby sees him.
**f** Diego is Aunt May's *cousin* / *neighbour*.
**g** Diego wants to go to the *national park* / *next town* with Abby.

## GUESS WHAT

**What happens in the next chapter? Tick the boxes.**

**a** Abby goes …
  1 ☐ into town with Aunt May for some new pants.
  2 ☐ to the national park with Diego.
  3 ☐ home to Dallas.

**b** Abby gives a sudden cry because …
  1 ☐ she is excited by something.
  2 ☐ she is afraid of something.
  3 ☐ something hits her.

**c** Abby and Bianca want to …
  1 ☐ stay at home.
  2 ☐ have a picnic.
  3 ☐ pick up garbage.

**d** Abby can't sleep at night because …
  1 ☐ Aunt May watches television in bed for hours.
  2 ☐ the neighbours are making a noise.
  3 ☐ it's raining very noisily.

**e** Abby talks late at night to …
  1 ☐ Aunt May.
  2 ☐ Diego.
  3 ☐ her mom and dad on the phone.

**f** Abby isn't happy …
  1 ☐ with her old friends in Dallas.
  2 ☐ at school.
  3 ☐ with her mom and dad.

That evening, Abby tells her aunt, 'Sorry about earlier. Can I visit the national park tomorrow – with Diego and his cousin?' '**Sure**,' Aunt May smiles.

Next day, Bianca takes Diego and Abby to **Point Reyes** national park. They see a lot of animals.

When they're walking there, Abby suddenly cries, 'Ugh ... there's something on me!'

'It's a beautiful **beetle**,' Bianca says. Abby looks down at the beetle. 'Well, it *is* a nice colour,' she thinks.

**sure** when you want to say 'yes' to somebody you say this

**Point Reyes** /ˌpɔɪnt ˈreɪjez/

**beetle** a small animal with a hard body and wings

Abby has a good time at the park. 'Do you want to come again? We can have a **picnic** next time,' Bianca says. 'OK, but when?' Abby asks.

It's a **windy** evening when Abby comes home. 'Nice day?' Aunt May asks. 'Yes,' Abby answers, 'and we're having a picnic at Point Reyes tomorrow.'

**picnic** when you eat out in the country, often sitting on the ground

**windy** when the air moves fast

That night, there's a **storm.** Abby can't sleep. She gets up for some water. Just then, Aunt May comes in and finds her. 'What's the matter?' she asks. 'Well ...' begins Abby.

They sit at the table. Abby plays with the pebbles there, and speaks about her **parents**.

**storm** when the weather is bad with a lot of rain and wind

**parents** mother and father

'Dad's always working, and Mom doesn't like my friends,' she says. 'Talk to them,' Aunt May tells her. 'How can I?' Abby answers.

10

# ACTIVITIES

## READING CHECK

**Correct these sentences.**

*Abby*

**a** ~~Diego~~ says 'sorry' to Aunt May.

**b** Bianca doesn't like the beetle.

**c** Point Reyes isn't very nice, Abby thinks.

**d** Abby wants to have breakfast at Point Reyes the next day.

**e** Abby can't sleep at night because there's a plane in the sky.

**f** Abby plays with some beetles in the kitchen.

**g** Abby tells Aunt May about her friends.

**h** Abby's mom is always working.

## GUESS WHAT

**What happens in the next chapter? Tick two pictures.**

**a** ☐

**b** ☐

**c** ☐

**d** ☐

## Chapter 4

**A ship on the rocks**

Next morning, Abby and her aunt are watching TV.

A **reporter** is talking. 'Today – after last night's storm – there's a **ship** on the **rocks** at Point Reyes, and a lot of **oil** in the water,' the reporter says.

Diego and Bianca arrive at Aunt May's house.
'No picnic today,' Abby says.
'Not with that **oil spill**,' Diego **agrees**. 'But maybe we can help. We must go and see!'

**reporter**  this person speaks on TV about new and interesting things

**ship**  you use a ship to go across the water

**rock**  a very big stone

**oil**  this is black, and we can burn it

**oil spill**  when oil goes from a ship into the sea or onto a beach

**agree**  to say what other people are saying

When they arrive at Point Reyes, there's oil on the beach. Diego and Abby see a lot of dead birds.

The **mayor** is talking to a reporter. 'Neighbours from villages near here must help,' he says. 'We're having a **meeting** this afternoon.'

'Look at the beach!' Abby cries. 'What can we do?'
'Let's go to the meeting and see,' Bianca answers.

**mayor** the most important man in a town

**meeting** when a number of people come to talk about something important

There are a lot of people at the meeting.

'**Teams** of people can pick up the oil,' the mayor says.
'But how do we move the ship?' a man asks.
'I don't know,' the mayor answers. 'Ask that man there. He's from the oil **company**.'

DeepOil

'DeepOil can't move the ship,' the oil man says. 'It's our oil. But it isn't our ship, you see.'
'DeepOil's my dad's company!' Abby says.

**team** a number of people who work together

**company** a group of people all working to make or do something for money

## READING CHECK

**Put the events in order.**

**a** They see oil and dead birds there when they arrive. ☐

**b** Diego and Bianca arrive at Aunt May's house. ☐

**c** Abby and Aunt May watch the reporter on TV. ☐

**d** A ship hits the rocks at Point Reyes. ☐

**e** Abby, her aunt, and friends go to the beach. ☐

**f** The mayor is speaking to a TV reporter about a meeting. ☐

**g** Abby hears the name of her dad's oil company. ☐

**h** Abby, her aunt, and friends go to the meeting. ☐

## GUESS WHAT

**What happens in the next chapter? Tick one box each in a, b, c, and d.**

**a** Aunt May ...

1 ☐ talks to Abby about calling her dad.

2 ☐ calls Abby's mom.

3 ☐ calls Abby's dad.

**b** Abby ...

1 ☐ goes back to Dallas.

2 ☐ visits Dubai.

3 ☐ asks her dad for something.

**c** Abby's dad ...

1 ☐ comes to Point Reyes.

2 ☐ talks to Abby on the phone.

3 ☐ leaves Dubai at once.

**d** Diego and Bianca ...

1 ☐ help down at the beach.

2 ☐ visit Aunt May's house.

3 ☐ speak to people from DeepOil.

# Chapter 5  A call for help

After the meeting, Aunt May tells Abby, '*I* can't call your father. We don't **get on**. *You* must do it.'
'But Dad never listens to me,' Abby cries.
'You can change things,' her aunt says. **'Believe** me.'
'She's right,' Abby thinks. So she calls.

In Dubai, Abby's dad is sleeping when the phone **rings**. 'Uhh ... It's 4:00 a.m. here!' he says. 'What is it, Abby?'
'Sorry, Dad,' Abby says. 'I need your help.'

**get on**  to feel OK with someone

**believe**  to think that someone or something is true

**ring**  to make a noise like a bell

She tells him about the ship on the rocks and the oil spill. He listens.
'Talk to people in your company, Dad!' she says. 'Please **persuade** them. They must help.'
'OK,' he answers.

After the phone call, Abby tells her aunt, 'He's talking to people at DeepOil. It's working!'
'You see!' Aunt May says.

**persuade** to make someone change their thinking by speaking to them

Next morning ...

Bianca and Diego are **cleaning** the beach when Abby and Aunt May arrive.

They work all day ... and all week!

One day, Abby and Diego are cleaning birds. 'There's oil all over me. But I'm OK with that,' Abby thinks. 'I can't believe it!'

After work, her phone rings.
'Abby, your mom and I are in Dallas,' her dad says. 'You can come home!'
'Oh, Dad!' Abby cries.

**clean** to stop something being dirty

## READING CHECK

**Tick the correct ending to complete each sentence.**

**a** Aunt May doesn't want to phone Abby's dad because …
1 ☐ he's always working.
2 ☑ they don't get on.

**b** When Abby phones, her dad is …
1 ☐ in a meeting.
2 ☐ in bed.

**c** Abby's dad can …
1 ☐ talk to DeepOil company people.
2 ☐ come to Point Reyes.

**d** Abby and Diego …
1 ☐ persuade the oil company.
2 ☐ clean the beach.

**e** Abby is OK about …
1 ☐ the oil on her.
2 ☐ the dead birds.

**f** Some days later, Abby's dad calls her from …
1 ☐ Dubai.
2 ☐ Dallas.

## GUESS WHAT

**What happens in the next chapter? Tick two boxes to finish each sentence.**

**a** DeepOil …
1 sends a team of its people to Point Reyes. ☐
2 helps to clean the beach. ☐
3 has a meeting with the mayor. ☐

**b** Abby and Diego …
1 help at the beach all summer. ☐
2 go to Dallas for a vacation. ☐
3 learn a lot about animals. ☐

**c** In the end, Abby is happy to …
1 go to school in California. ☐
2 visit her aunt again. ☐
3 go back home to Dallas. ☐

Abby listens to her phone. 'Everybody here in the Dallas office agrees,' her dad says. 'A DeepOil team's coming to Point Reyes.'

'That's wonderful!' Abby cries happily. 'Hey, take it easy! They can't **empty** the ship in a day!' her dad says. 'So can I stay here for longer?' she asks. 'Sure!' her dad answers.

**empty** to take things out of something so it has nothing in it

Next week, the DeepOil team arrives and begins work. Abby and Diego help at the beach for weeks.

After work, the two of them visit the national park. They learn about the animals there from Bianca.

But then the summer finishes, and Abby's vacation finishes, too.

At the airport, Aunt May gives a **heavy** little bag to Abby. Diego gives a picture of a **whale** to her.

'Can you see whales here?' Abby asks Diego.
'In the **spring**,' he answers.

**heavy**  not easy to pick up

**whale**  a very big animal that lives in the sea and looks like a fish

**spring**  the three months of the year before summer when it is warm

21

Abby's dad meets her in Dallas. 'Sorry about your vacation,' he says. 'Why?' Abby laughs. 'I get on with Aunt May. I want to visit her again next spring.'

At home, Abby empties her aunt's heavy little bag on the table. 'Every pebble's different,' she tells her parents.

Her mom smiles. Her dad laughs. And Abby laughs, too. Suddenly it's good to be home.

## READING CHECK

**1 Tick the correct people.**

**Who ...**

**a** ... wants to visit California in the spring?

**1**  **2**  □ □

**b** ... teaches Abby and Diego a lot?

**1**  **2**  □ □

**c** ... takes a heavy bag home?

**1**  **2**  □ □

**d** ... gives a picture to Abby?

**1**  **2**  □ □

**2 Correct the sentences.**

**a** The Dallas DeepOil office sends a ~~ship~~ team to Point Reyes.

**b** Abby and Diego sleep at the beach for some weeks.

**c** When the vacation finishes, Aunt May and Diego go to the hotel with Abby.

**d** Visitors to Point Reyes in the summer can see whales there.

**e** Abby's dad is sorry about Abby's pants.

**f** Abby wants to stay with Cousin Bianca next year.

**g** Abby is afraid at home in the end.

## GUESS WHAT?

**What happens after the story ends? Answer the questions.**

**a** Where does Abby go in the spring?

**b** What does Abby give to Sadie?

**c** Who does Diego email every day?

**d** Why does Aunt May phone Abby's dad?

## Project A  *Writing and performing a dialogue*

**1  Complete this dialogue between Abby and Diego. Use the words in the box.**

> animals   How   neighbours   What   Why   garbage   staying   kills   house

**Abby**   **a)**................ are you putting in that bag?

**Diego**   It's **b)**................ . I'm picking it up.

**Abby**   **c)**................ are you doing that?

**Diego**   It's very bad for **d)**................ . When they eat it, it **e)**................ them.

**Abby**   Oh. Right.

**Diego**   I know you. You're **f)**................ in May Wilson's **g)**................ .

**Abby**   Yes. **h)**................ do you know that?

**Diego**   Because we're **i)**................ !

**2  Complete the dialogue with Diego's answers in the box.**

**Abby**   Do you know about the ship on the rocks at Point Reyes?

**Diego**   **a)**................ .

**Abby**   So we can't have a picnic there now.

**Diego**   **b)**................ .

**Abby**   Well then, what do you want to do today?

**Diego**   **c)**................ .

**Abby**   Go to Point Reyes? Why?

**Diego**   **d)**................ .

**Abby**   But how can we help?

**Diego**   **e)**................ .

**Abby**   OK then.

**Diego**   **f)**................ .

> Come on. Bianca's waiting. Let's go.
>
> Because maybe we can help.
>
> Yes. The oil's bad for the beach, Bianca says.
>
> No, not with all that oil on the beach.
>
> I don't know, but we must go and see.
>
> Want? You don't understand.
> We *must* go to the beach.

**3 Choose one of these pictures. Write a dialogue between the characters.**

...........................................................................................................

...........................................................................................................

...........................................................................................................

...........................................................................................................

...........................................................................................................

...........................................................................................................

...........................................................................................................

...........................................................................................................

...........................................................................................................

...........................................................................................................

**4 Perform your dialogue in class with a partner.**

## Project B — *A vacation blog*

**1** **Abby is writing a blog about her vacation. Find words in the story to complete her descriptions of the photos.**

### MY CALIFORNIA VACATION

This is the national **a)** . . . . . . . . . . . . . . . . at Point Reyes. My friend Diego's **b)** . . . . . . . . . . . . . . . . works here.

These are **c)** . . . . . . . . . . . . . . . . from the beach near my **d)** . . . . . . . . . . . . . . . . May's house.

Do you like this **e)** . . . . . . . . . . . . . . . . ? You can see them at Point Reyes. They're beautiful little **f)** . . . . . . . . . . . . . . . ., I think.

Here people are cleaning things after the **g)** . . . . . . . . . . . . . . . . . . . . . . . . . . . . . . near Point Reyes. Remember that? It isn't easy work – **h)** . . . . . . . . . . . . . . . . me!

**2** **Abby's parents are in Dubai. Check these words in a dictionary. Complete the descriptions of their photos.**

| beach | buy | tour | hotel | shopping mall | desert | buildings |

**a** This is the . . . . . . . . . . . . . . . . . in Dubai.

**b** Here's a . . . . . . . . . . . . . . . . . in Dubai. You can . . . . . . . . . . . . . . . . . most things here!

**c** This is our . . . . . . . . . . . . . . . . . of the . . . . . . . . . . . . . . . . . near Dubai. An interesting day out!

**d** Here are the tall . . . . . . . . . . . . . . . . . near our Dubai . . . . . . . . . . . . . . . . . – the Burj Khalifa!

**3** **Find photos of your last vacation. Write descriptions. Write a vacation blog. Use activities 1 and 2 to help you.**

**4** **Show and tell your class about your blog.**

## WORD WORK 1

**1 Complete the words from Chapters 1 and 2.**

**a** s u m m e r     **b** p _ bb _ _     **c** c _ n _ e _ t

**d** _ a _ n _     **e** p _ n _ s     **f** _ _ rb _ g _

**2 The red words are in the wrong sentences. Correct them.**

**a** May Wilson is Abby's **cousin**...... aunt ......

**b** Abby doesn't go to school in the summer **studio**...................

**c** 'Aunt May is **neighbours**,' Abby tells Sadie.................

**d** Aunt May is working on a picture in her **beach**...................

**e** Bianca is Diego's **aunt**...................

**f** The **vacation** at Point Reyes is beautiful...................

**g** Diego knows May Wilson because they are **crazy**...................

## WORD WORK 2

**1 Look at the pictures. Write the words from Chapters 3 and 4.**

a ....storm....

b ..................

c ..................

d ................

e ..................

f ..................

**2 Use the clues to complete the puzzle. What is the mystery name down?**

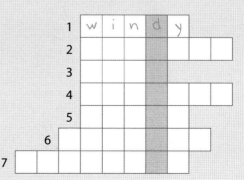

**1** when the air moves quickly

**2** your mom and dad

**3** when you want to say 'yes' to somebody, you say this

**4** a number of people all working for money

**5** an important man in a town

**6** when a lot of people come and talk about important things

**7** when oil goes into the sea

|  | 1 | w | i | n | d | y |  |  |
|---|---|---|---|---|---|---|---|---|
| 2 | | | | | | | | |
| 3 | | | | | | | | |
| 4 | | | | | | | | |
| 5 | | | | | | | | |
| 6 | | | | | | | | |
| 7 | | | | | | | | |

The mystery name down is: ..................

29

## WORD WORK 3

**1  Solve the anagrams on the pebbles to complete the sentences with words from Chapters 5 and 6.**

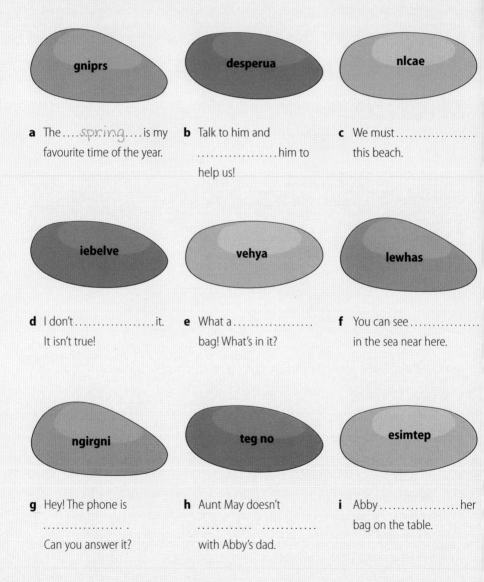

**gniprs**

**desperua**

**nlcae**

**a** The ....*spring*.... is my favourite time of the year.

**b** Talk to him and ................. him to help us!

**c** We must ................. this beach.

**iebelve**

**vehya**

**lewhas**

**d** I don't ................. it. It isn't true!

**e** What a ................. bag! What's in it?

**f** You can see ................. in the sea near here.

**ngirgni**

**teg no**

**esimtep**

**g** Hey! The phone is ................. . Can you answer it?

**h** Aunt May doesn't ............ ............ with Abby's dad.

**i** Abby ................. her bag on the table.

# GRAMMAR

## GRAMMAR CHECK

**must and can**

We use the modal auxiliary verb must to talk about strong obligation.
We use the modal auxiliary verb can to talk about ability or permission.

*'Maybe we can help. We must go and see!' (= can for ability; must for strong obligation)*

*DeepOil can't move the ship. (= can for ability)*

*'Can I visit the national park tomorrow – with Diego and his cousin?' (= can for permission)*

**1** **Circle the correct words to complete the sentences. Write the people saying them. Use some people more than once.**

| Sadie  the mayor  Abby's dad  Abby's mom  Abby  Aunt May  Diego |

**a** 'I *must* / can go to Dubai for three weeks', .Abby's.dad. says.

**b** 'You *must* / can't stay with my sister this summer', ................. tells her.

**c** 'Abby can / can't come to the concert. She's in California', ................. tells a friend.

**d** 'I *must* / can't go into town. Do you want to come?' ................. asks Abby.

**e** 'My cousin can / must take us to Point Reyes tomorrow', ................. tells Abby.

**f** 'Can / Must I go out tomorrow?' ................. asks Aunt May.

**g** 'I can't / can talk to my parents. They never listen to me!' ................. says.

**h** 'There's a town meeting this afternoon. Everyone must / can't come', ................. says.

**i** 'I must / can go back to Dallas because it's the end of the summer vacation', .................
tells Diego.

**j** 'Can / Must I visit Aunt May again next year?' ................. asks her parents.

**2** **The oil ship is on the rocks at Point Reyes. Complete the sentences with *must, can* or *can't*.**

**a** We .....can't..... save the ship! It's on the rocks and it's going down.

**b** ................. you see the oil in the water?

**c** Quick! We ................. drive to the national park now!

**d** The oil company ................. help us, they say. It isn't their ship.

**e** Everybody ................. help to clean the beach. It's important!

**f** ................. I ask the mayor a question about the oil spill?

**g** Abby, you ................. call your dad! Maybe he ................. do something.

**h** OK, Abby. I ................. speak to people in the company.

31

## GRAMMAR CHECK

### Present Continuous: present and future

We can use the Present Continuous to talk about actions in the present – now, or around now. We can use the Present Continuous to talk about plans for the future, too.

*'I'm Diego,' he says. 'And you're staying in May Wilson's house.'* (= action around now)

*'What are you doing?' she asks him.* (= action now)

*'I'm not going to the beach tomorrow.'* (= future plan)

*'Dad's working in Dubai for DeepOil for three weeks, and Mom's going with him.'* (= future plans)

We often use contractions with the verb be when we speak, or in informal writing.

*'I am = I'm, he is = he's, Dad is = Dad's, you are = you're*

**3** **Read the sentences. Write (P) next to the sentences about the present and (F) next to the sentences about the future.**

**a** Abby's parents are going to Dubai next week. [F]

**b** Aunt May is watching the TV now. ☐

**c** Look at that boy! He's picking up garbage. ☐

**d** DeepOil is sending a team to Point Reyes in a day or two. ☐

**e** There are people on the beach. They're cleaning the rocks. ☐

**f** I'm leaving for Dallas on Monday. ☐

**g** Dad's meeting me at the airport when I arrive. ☐

**4** **Complete the text with these verbs. Use the correct form of the present continuous.**

| come | do | go | help | learn | put | see | sit | take | teach | work |

After the oil spill, Abby **a)** ...*is sitting*... at her computer when Aunt May arrives. 'What **b)** .................. you .................. ?' Aunt May asks.

'I **c)** .................. photos of Point Reyes on my Facebook page,' Abby answers.

**d)** .................. you .................. to the beach today?'

'No,' Aunt May says. 'I **e)** .................. on a picture in my studio. And you?'

'Bianca and Diego **f)** .................. here at ten,' Abby answers. 'We **g)** .................. at the beach this morning. Then Bianca **h)** .................. us to the national park. She **i)** .................. us all about the animals there. I **j)** .................. a lot.'

'You **k)** .................. a lot of Bianca and Diego these days!' Aunt May says.

## GRAMMAR CHECK

### Articles: a / an and the

We use the indefinite article a / an before singular nouns when we talk about them for the first time. We use a before a consonant sound and an before a vowel sound.

We use the definite article the before singular nouns when we know the thing we are talking about, or when there is only one of something.

*There's an oil spill on the beach.*

*Diego gives a picture of a whale to Abby.*

*Bianca teaches them about all the animals in the national park.*

**5** Circle the correct words to complete the sentences.

**a** Aunt May lives in (a) / the little town near the / a Pacific Ocean.

**b** She drives a / an old Beetle. Everyone in a / the town knows the / a car.

**c** Aunt May is an / a interesting woman. She has a / an big studio with a lot of pictures in it.

**d** When Aunt May isn't working on a / the picture, she likes to walk on a / the beach.

**e** Aunt May often picks up pebbles from a / the beach. She puts them all over the / a house.

**f** Aunt May has a / an younger sister. Her sister lives in an / a expensive house in Dallas.

**6** Complete the text with *a*, *an* or *the*.

When Dad meets Abby at **a)** ......the...... airport, she's carrying **b)** .................. old bag. He puts **c)** .................. bag into **d)** .................. car. 'What's that?' he asks. 'Something from Aunt May,' Abby says.

At home, Abby puts **e)** .................. bag on **f)** .................. table and opens it. She picks up **g)** .................. interesting pebble and says, 'It's **h)** .................. wonderful thing. Every pebble is different, you know.'

# DOMINOES Your Choice

Read *Dominoes* for pleasure, or to develop language skills. It's your choice.

Each *Domino* reader includes:
- a good story to enjoy
- integrated activities to develop reading skills and increase vocabulary
- task-based projects – perfect for CEFR portfolios
- contextualized grammar activities

Each *Domino* pack contains a reader, and an excitingly dramatized audio recording of the story

If you liked this *Domino*, read these:

### Lisa's Song
*by Lesley Thompson*

Al Brown plays the guitar in a band with friends. He writes songs, too. 'Our boy can't live without his music,' his parents say.

But when Al's baby sister, Lisa, arrives from hospital, his life is suddenly different. Now his mother and father have no time for him, and he has no time for school work – or the band.

Then Al's sister gets ill. And Grandad tells him, 'Write a song for Lisa!' But why, and how can this help?

### The Skateboarder
*by Chris Lindop*

'I love Owen's skateboarding,' Hannah thinks. 'I want to jump and do tricks, too.'

When a skatepark opens near her house, Hannah is suddenly very interested in skateboarding. How do Mom, Dad, brother Evan, and cousin Justin feel about this? Who helps her? Who laughs at her? And who teaches her to be a real skateboarder in the end? This story has the answers.

|  | CEFR | Cambridge Exams | IELTS | TOEFL iBT | TOEIC |
|---|---|---|---|---|---|
| Level 3 | B1 | PET | 4.0 | 57–86 | 550 |
| Level 2 | A2–B1 | KET–PET | 3.0–4.0 | – | 390 |
| Level 1 | A1–A2 | YLE Flyers/KET | 3.0 | – | 225 |
| Starter & Quick Starter | A1 | YLE Movers | 1.0–2.0 | – | – |

You can find details and a full list of books and teachers' resources on our website:
www.oup.com/elt/gradedreaders